Menieres Disease Art Therapy

Healing Garden

Butterflies And Flower Gardens

Stress Relief and Relaxation To Promote Healing

charlotte berry

BIC Subject category: 1. Drawing-coloring books for grown-ups 2. Arts & Photography- techniques
3. Craft, hobbies- art 4. Self-help-art therapy & relaxation 5. Self-help-anger management. 6.Self-help-stress relief

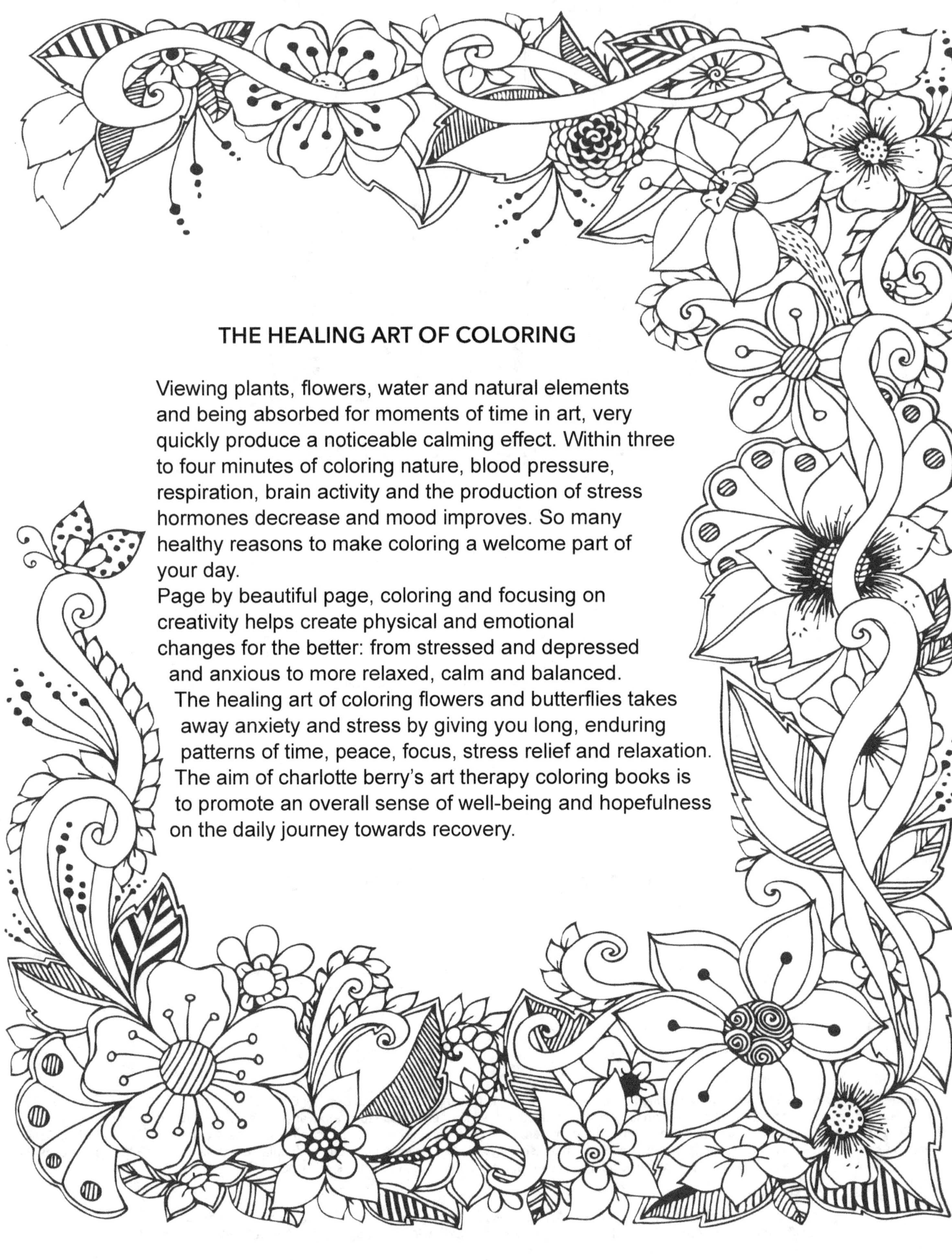

THE HEALING ART OF COLORING

Viewing plants, flowers, water and natural elements
and being absorbed for moments of time in art, very
quickly produce a noticeable calming effect. Within three
to four minutes of coloring nature, blood pressure,
respiration, brain activity and the production of stress
hormones decrease and mood improves. So many
healthy reasons to make coloring a welcome part of
your day.

Page by beautiful page, coloring and focusing on
creativity helps create physical and emotional
changes for the better: from stressed and depressed
and anxious to more relaxed, calm and balanced.
The healing art of coloring flowers and butterflies takes
away anxiety and stress by giving you long, enduring
patterns of time, peace, focus, stress relief and relaxation.
The aim of charlotte berry's art therapy coloring books is
to promote an overall sense of well-being and hopefulness
on the daily journey towards recovery.

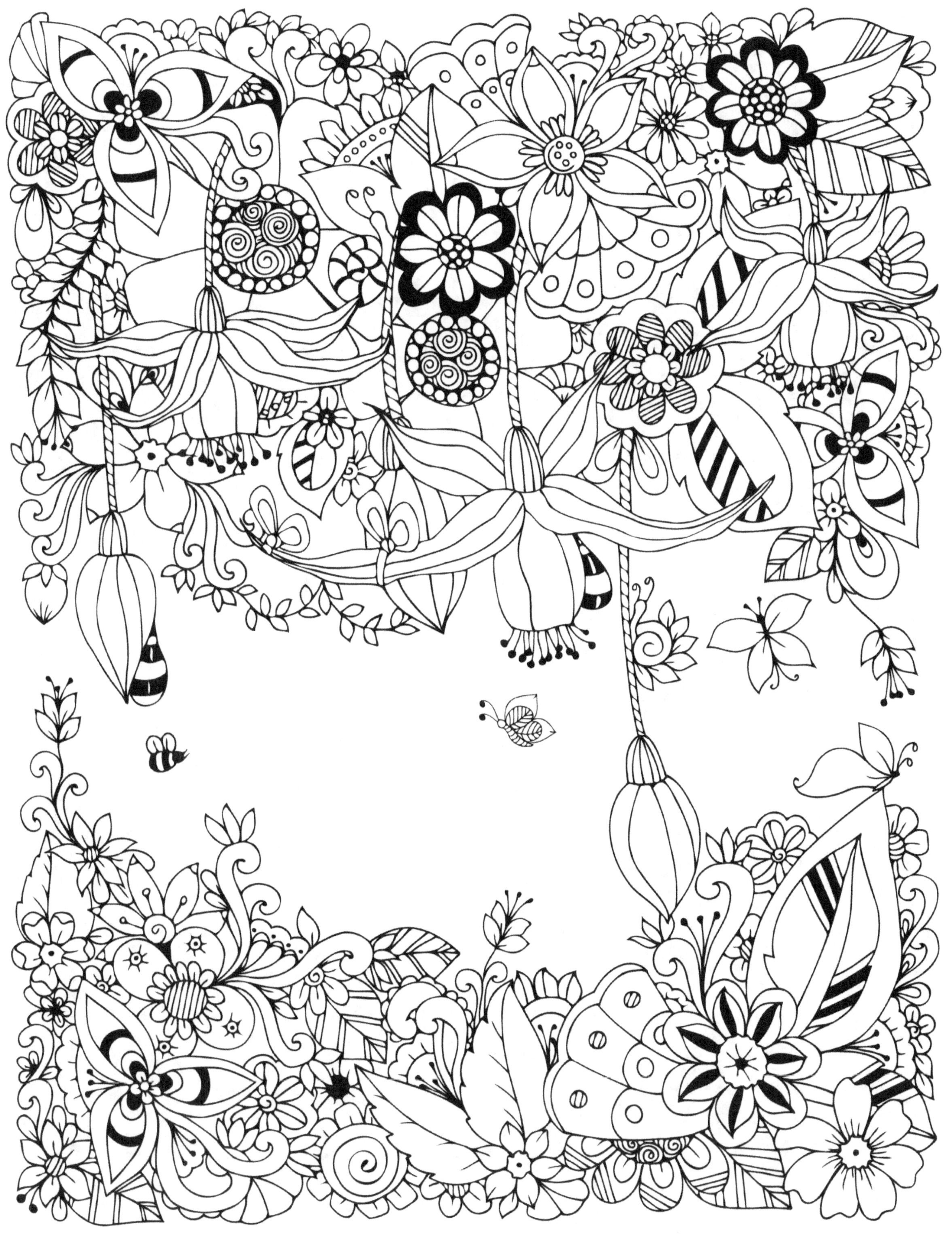

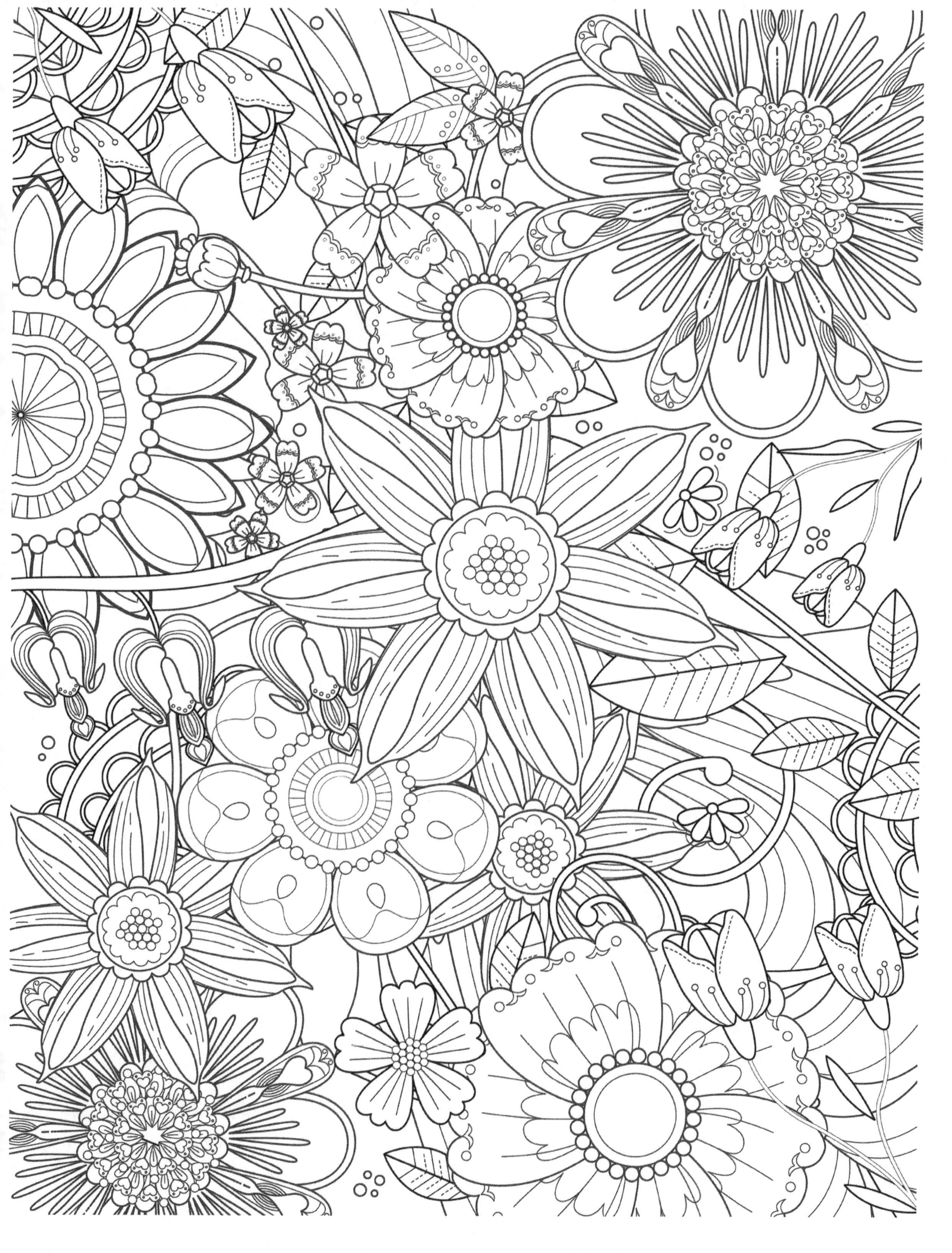

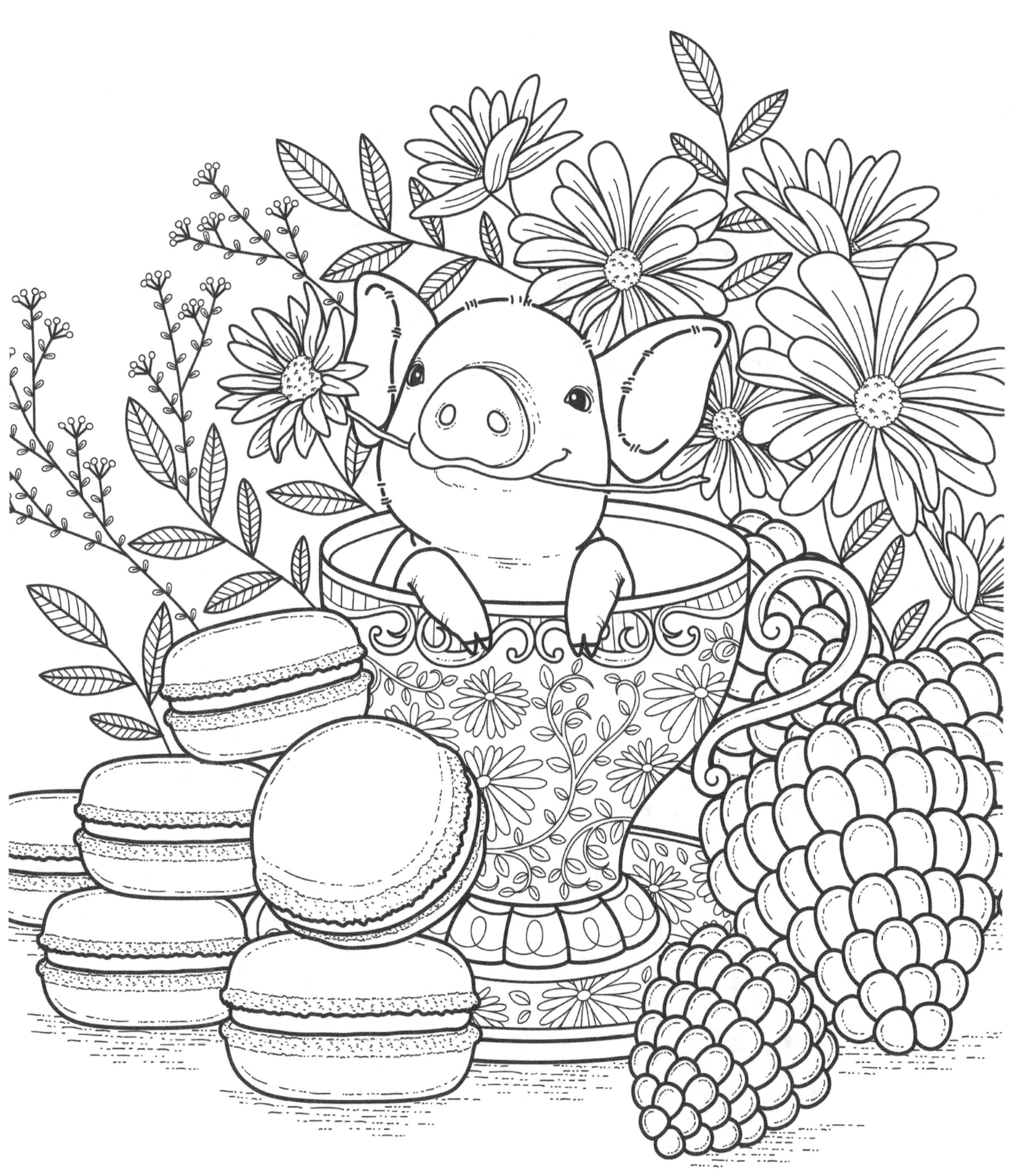

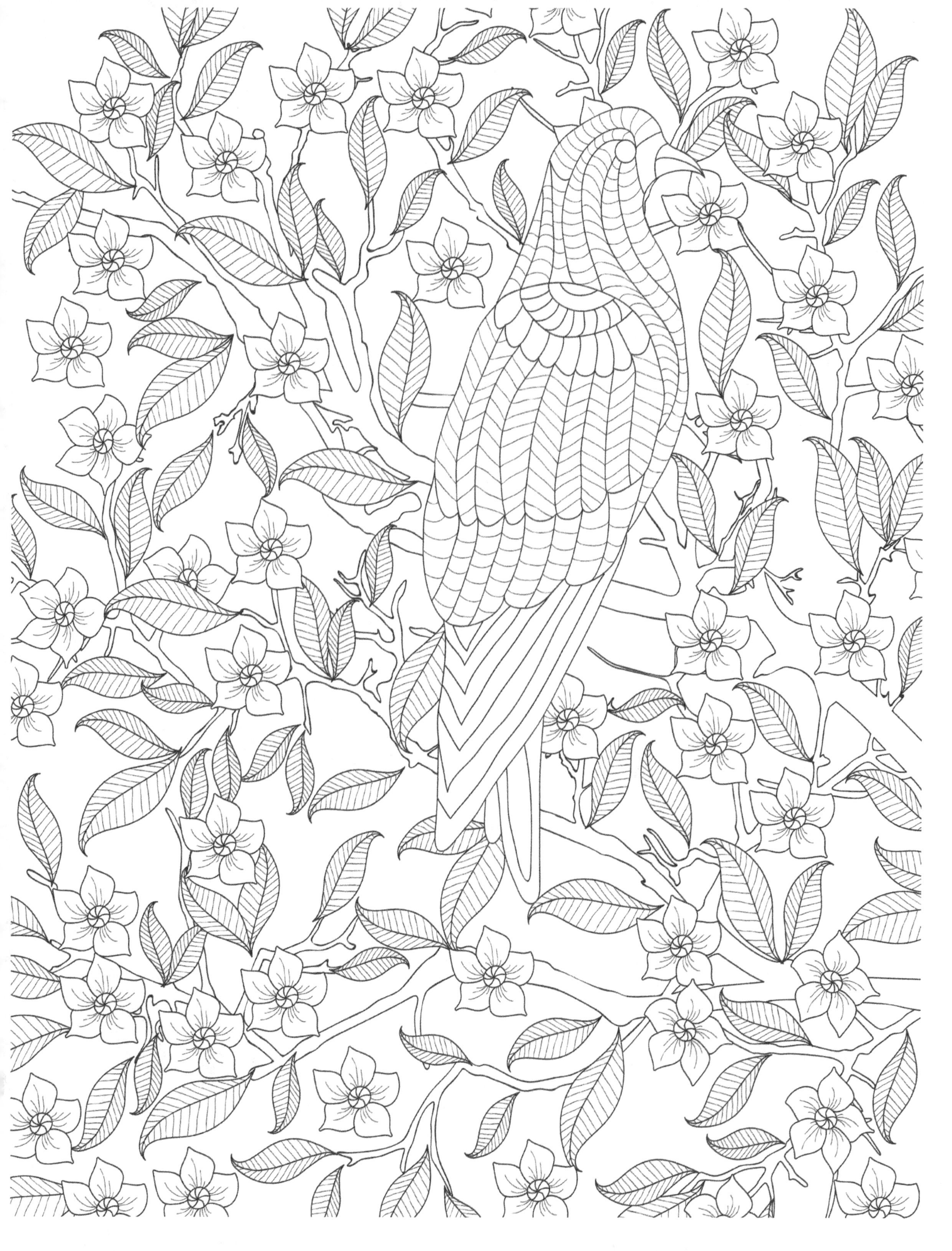

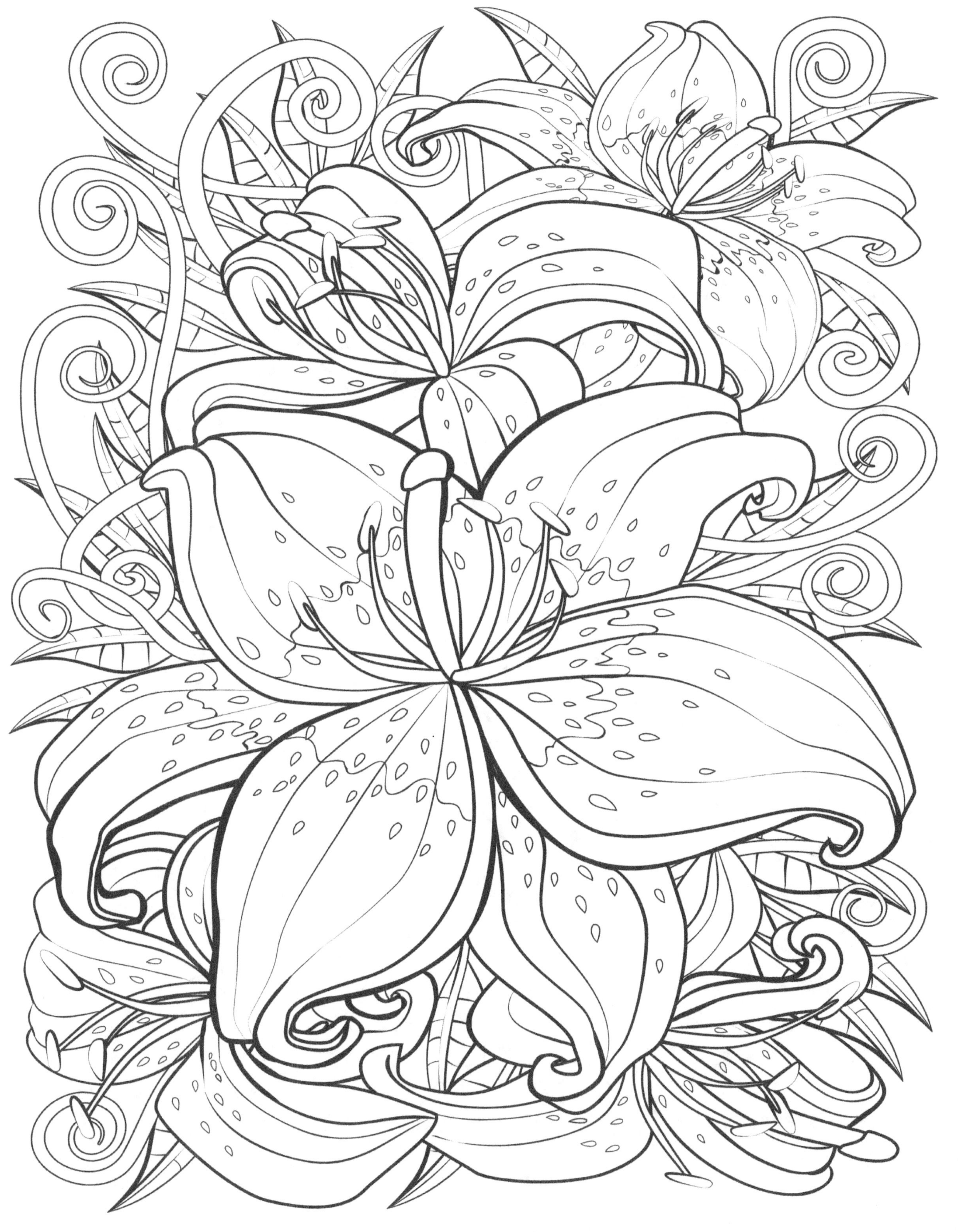

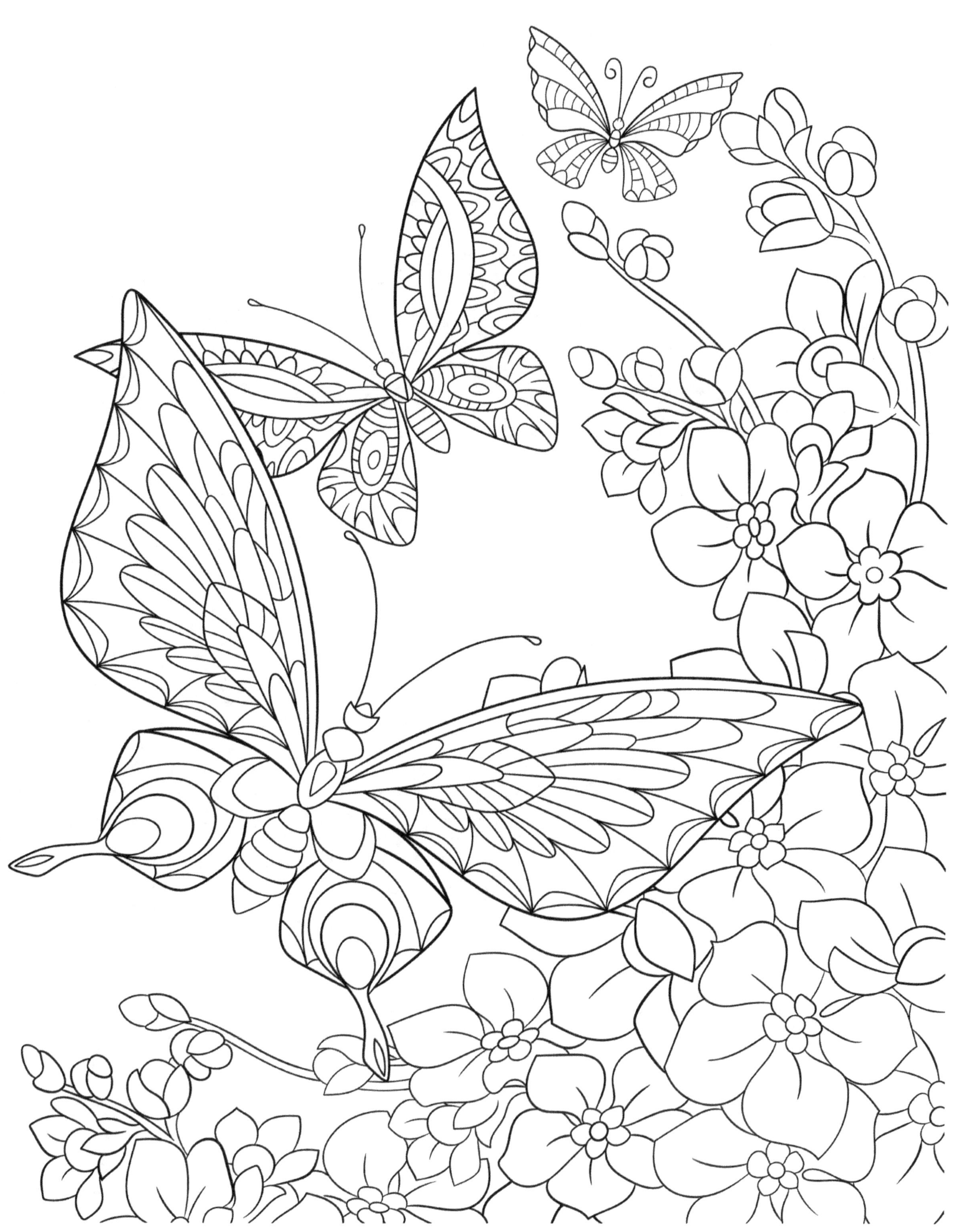

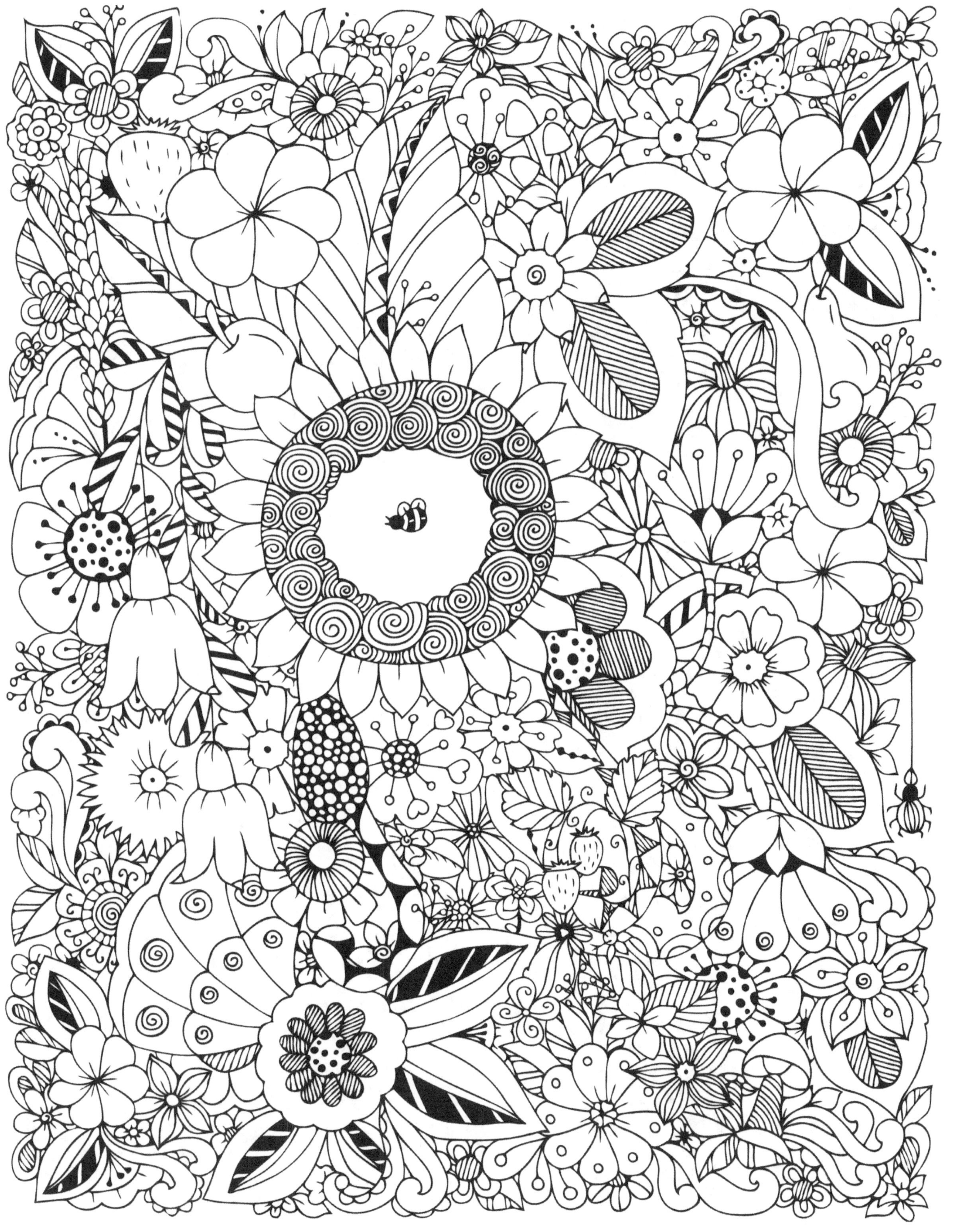

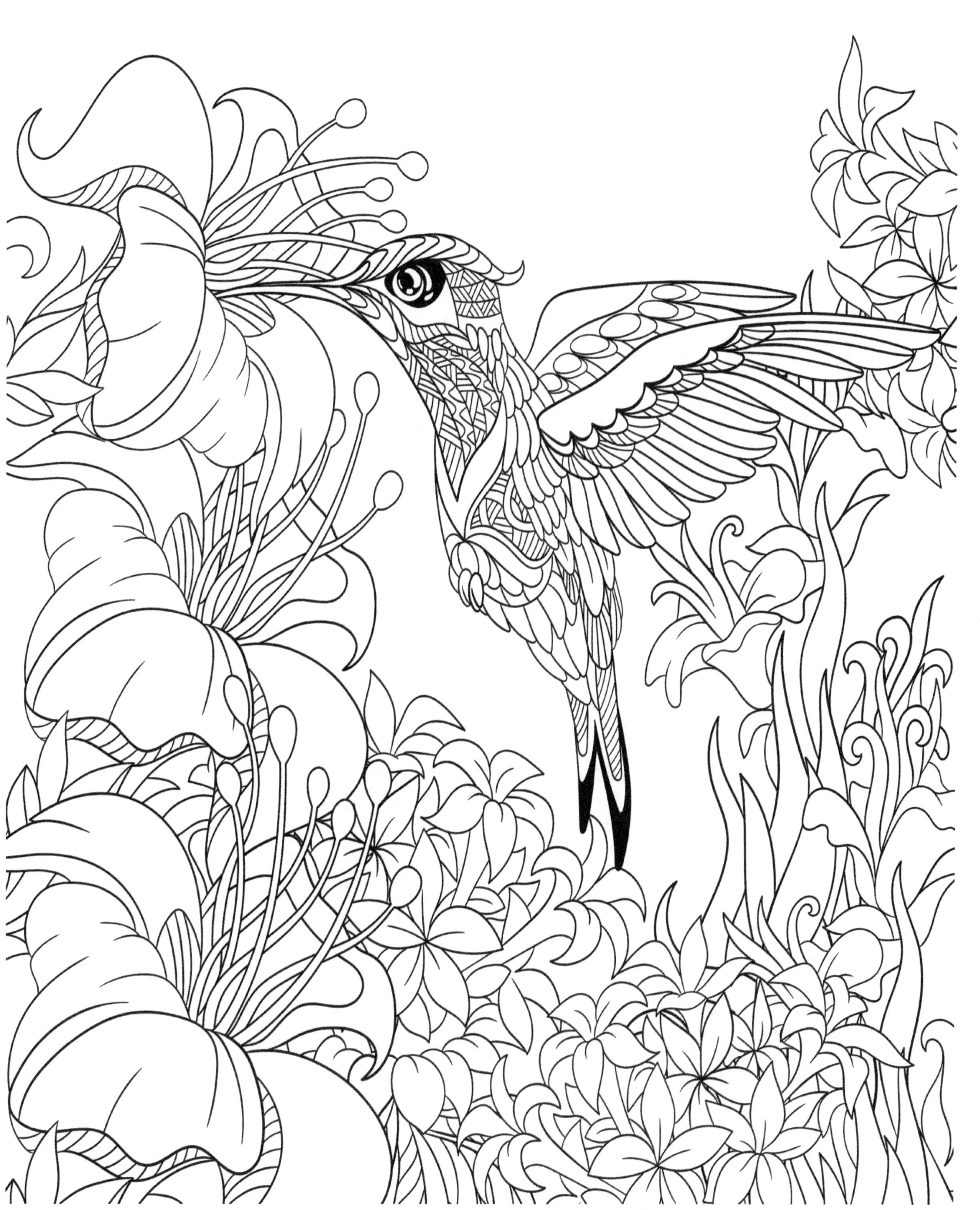

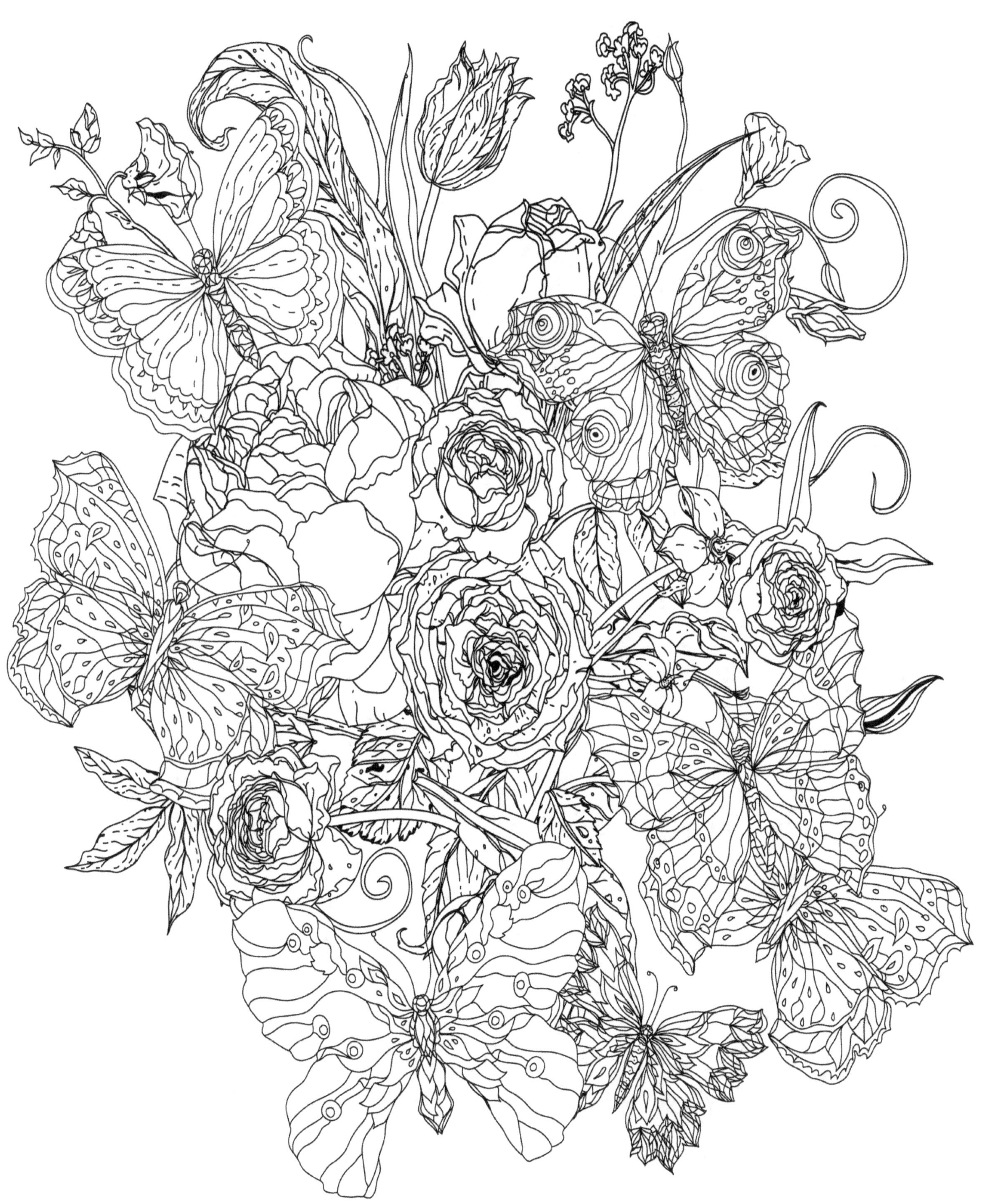

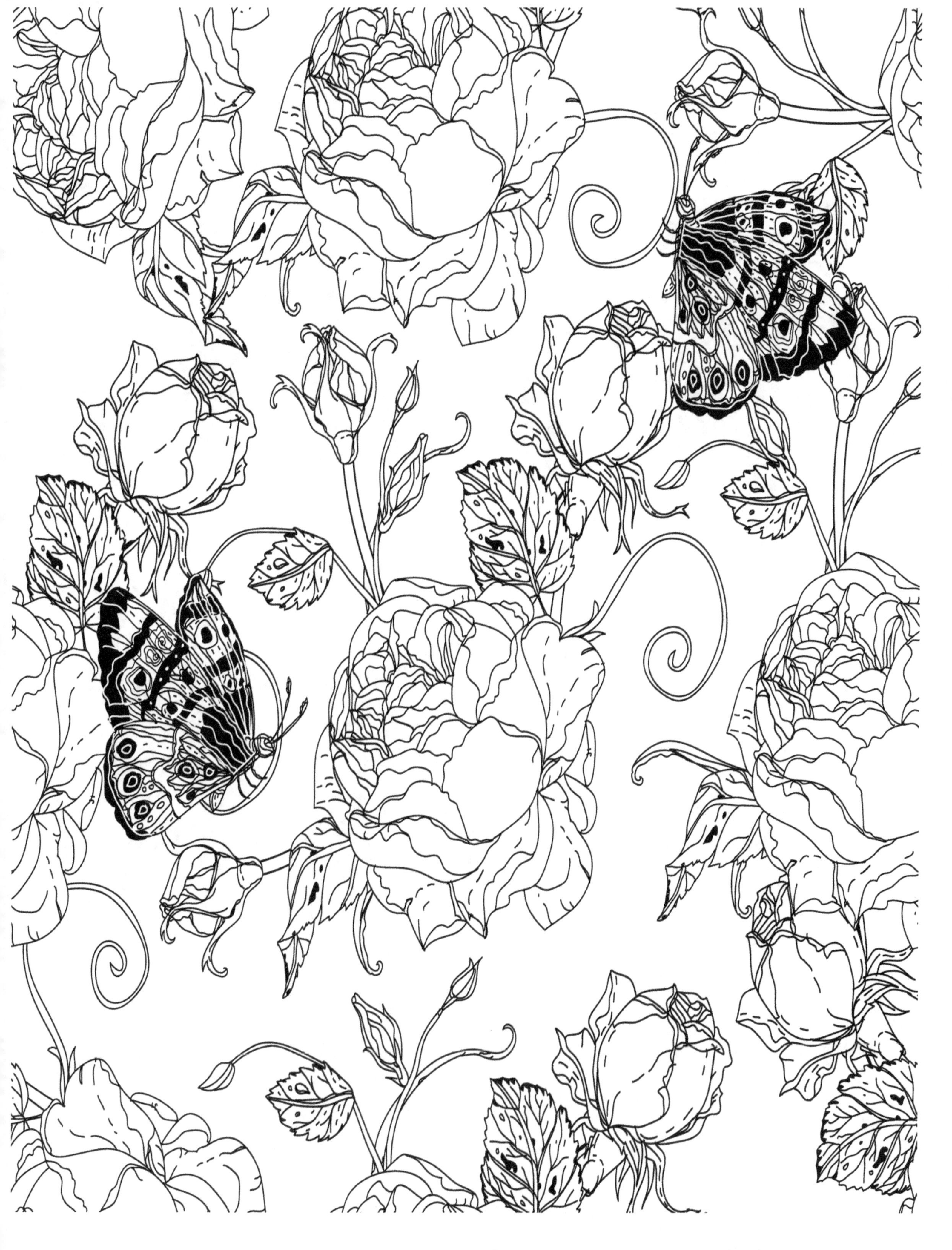

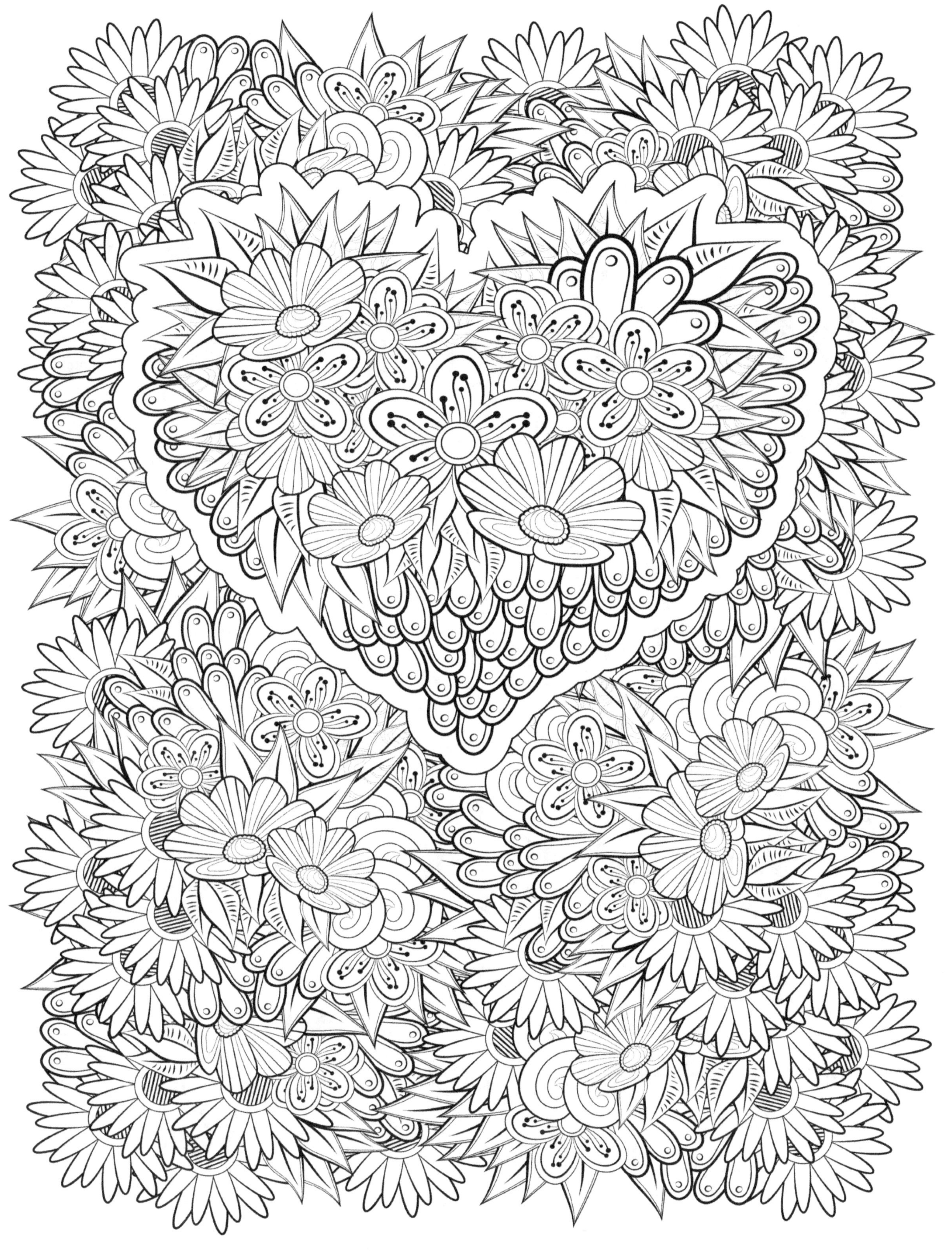

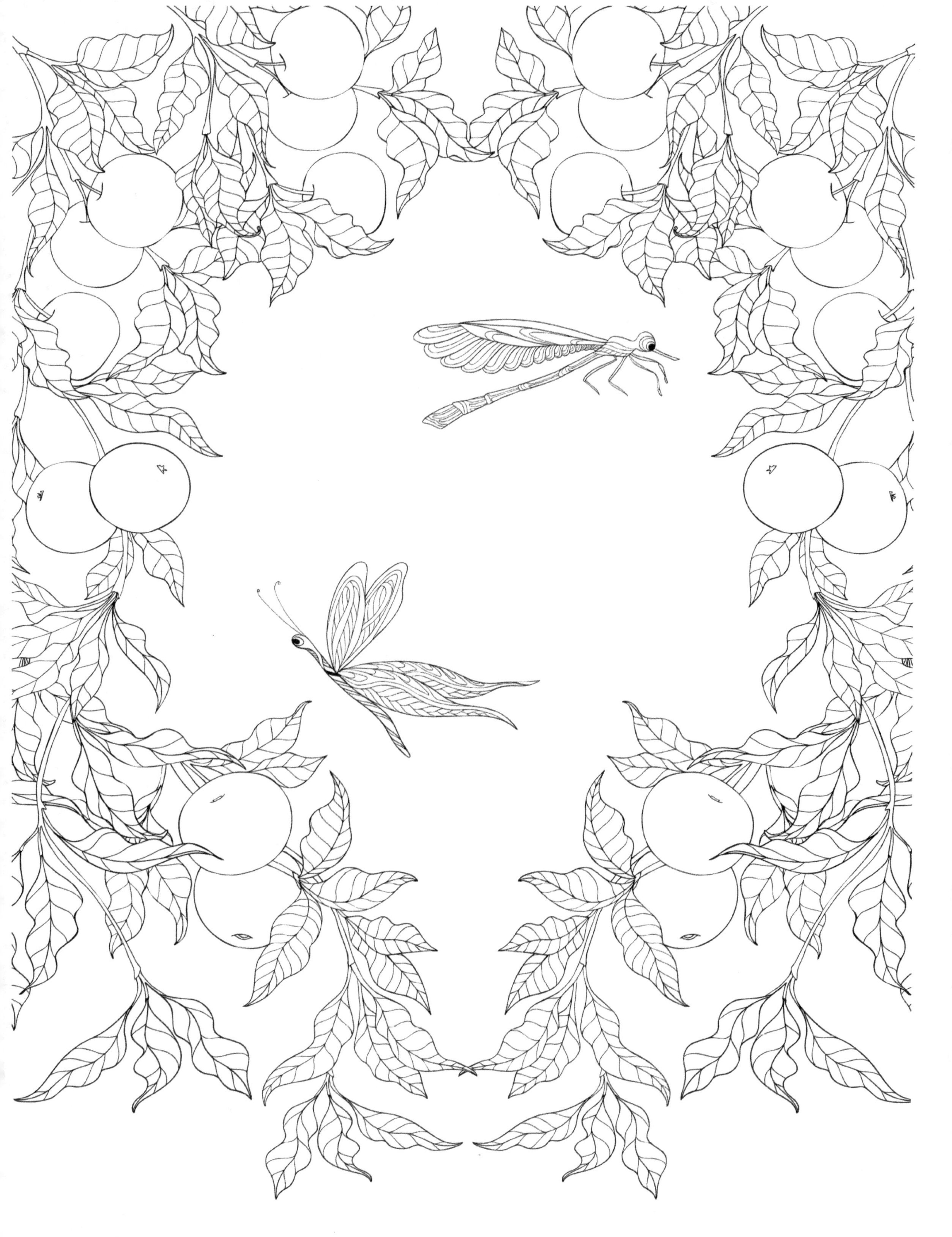

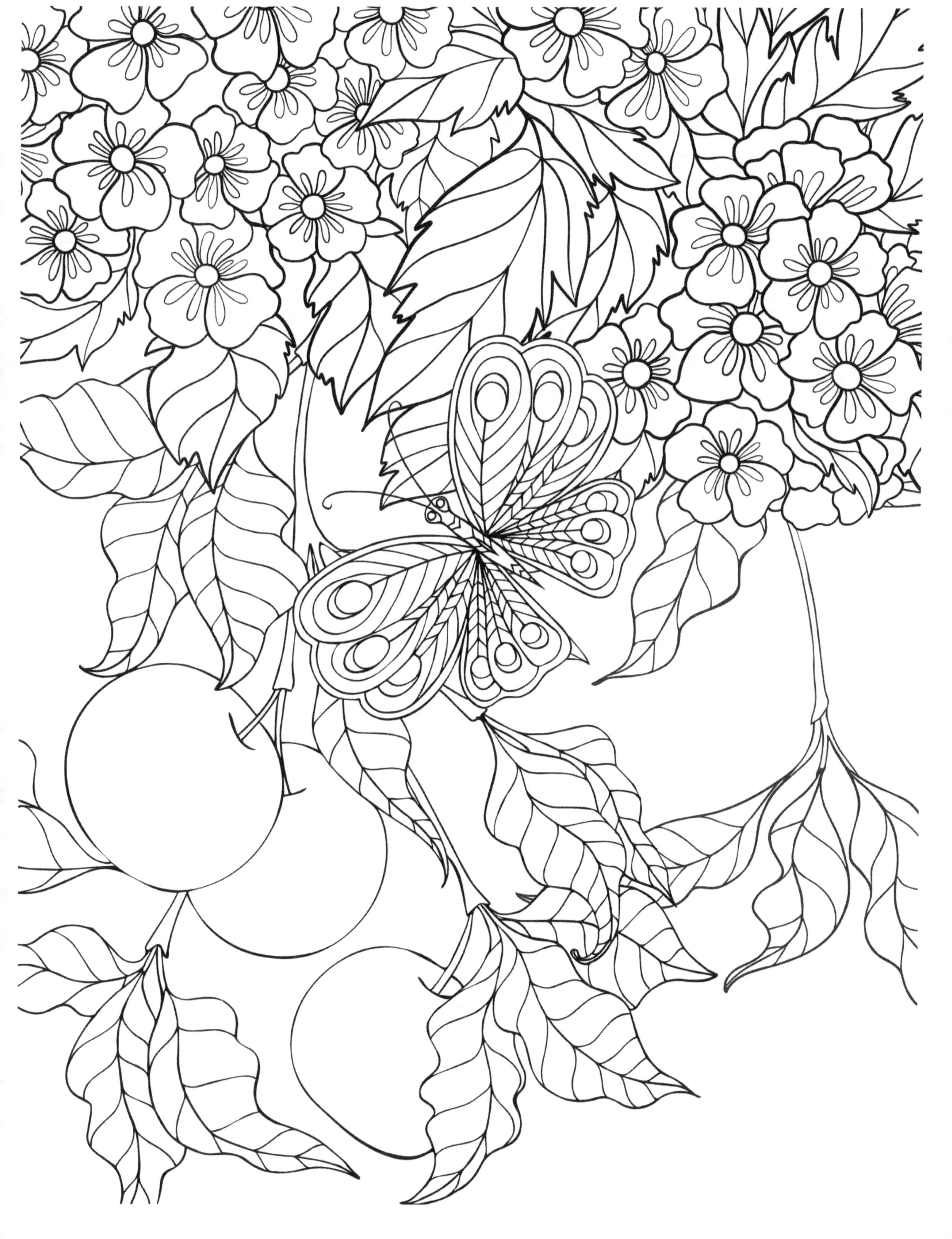

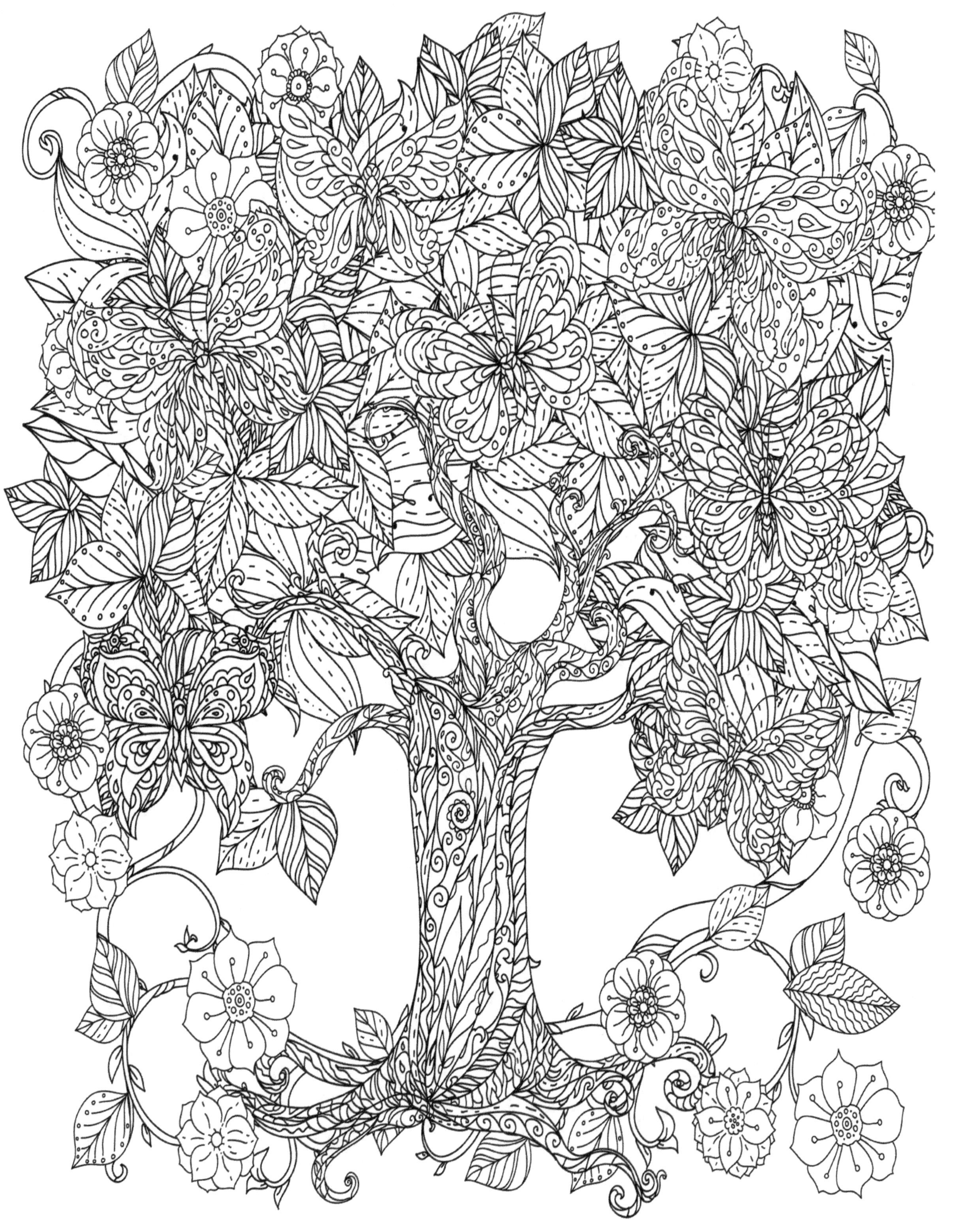

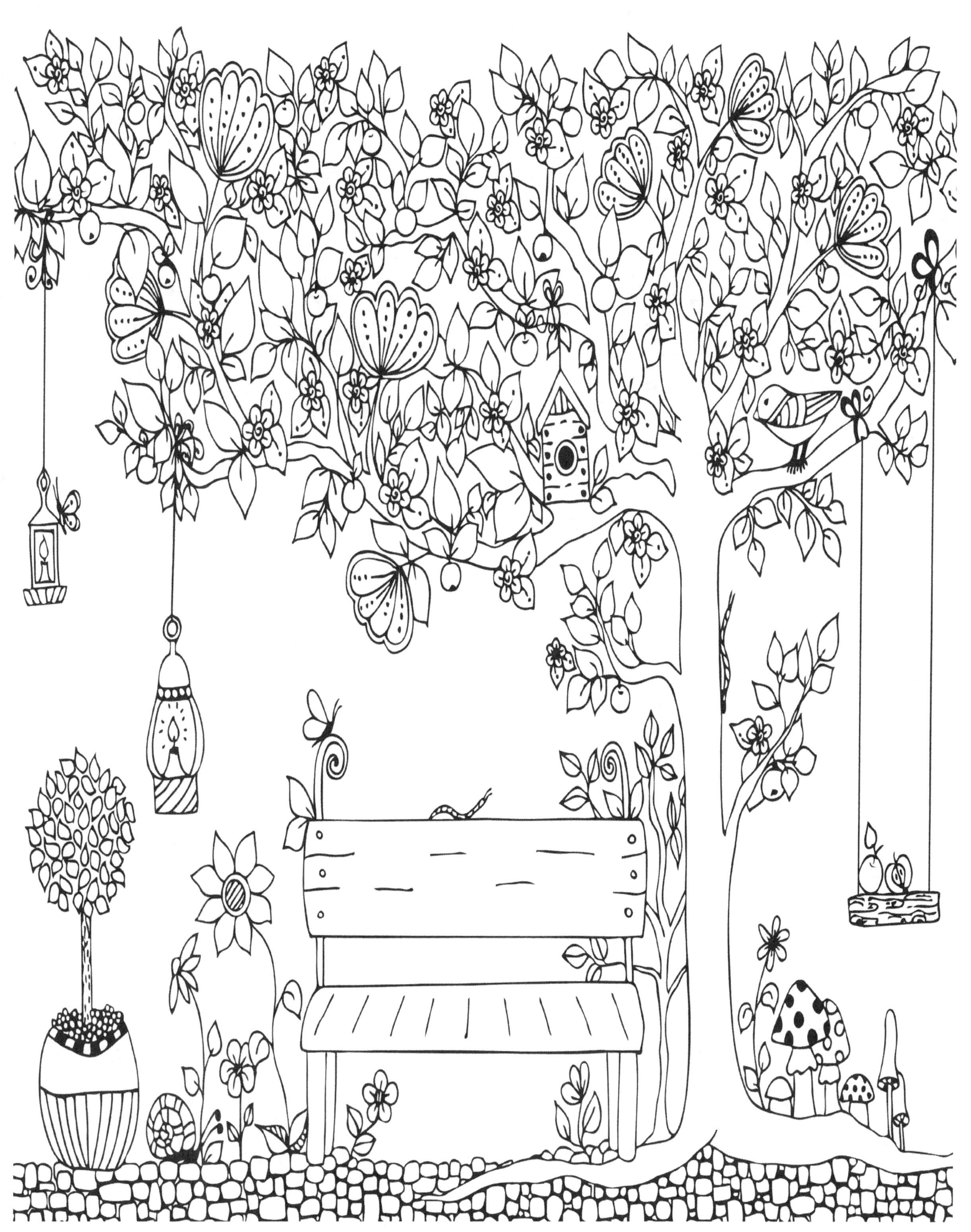

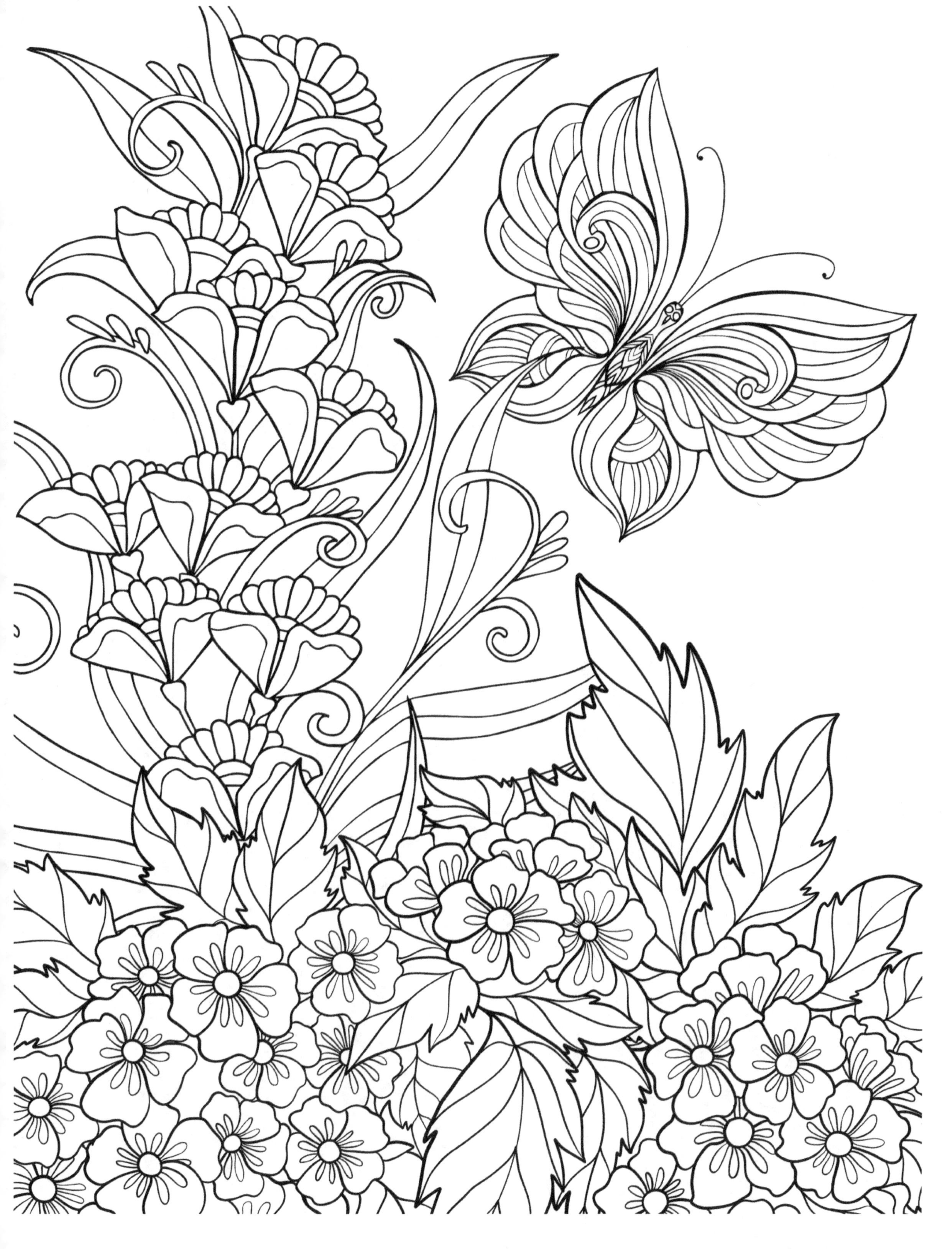

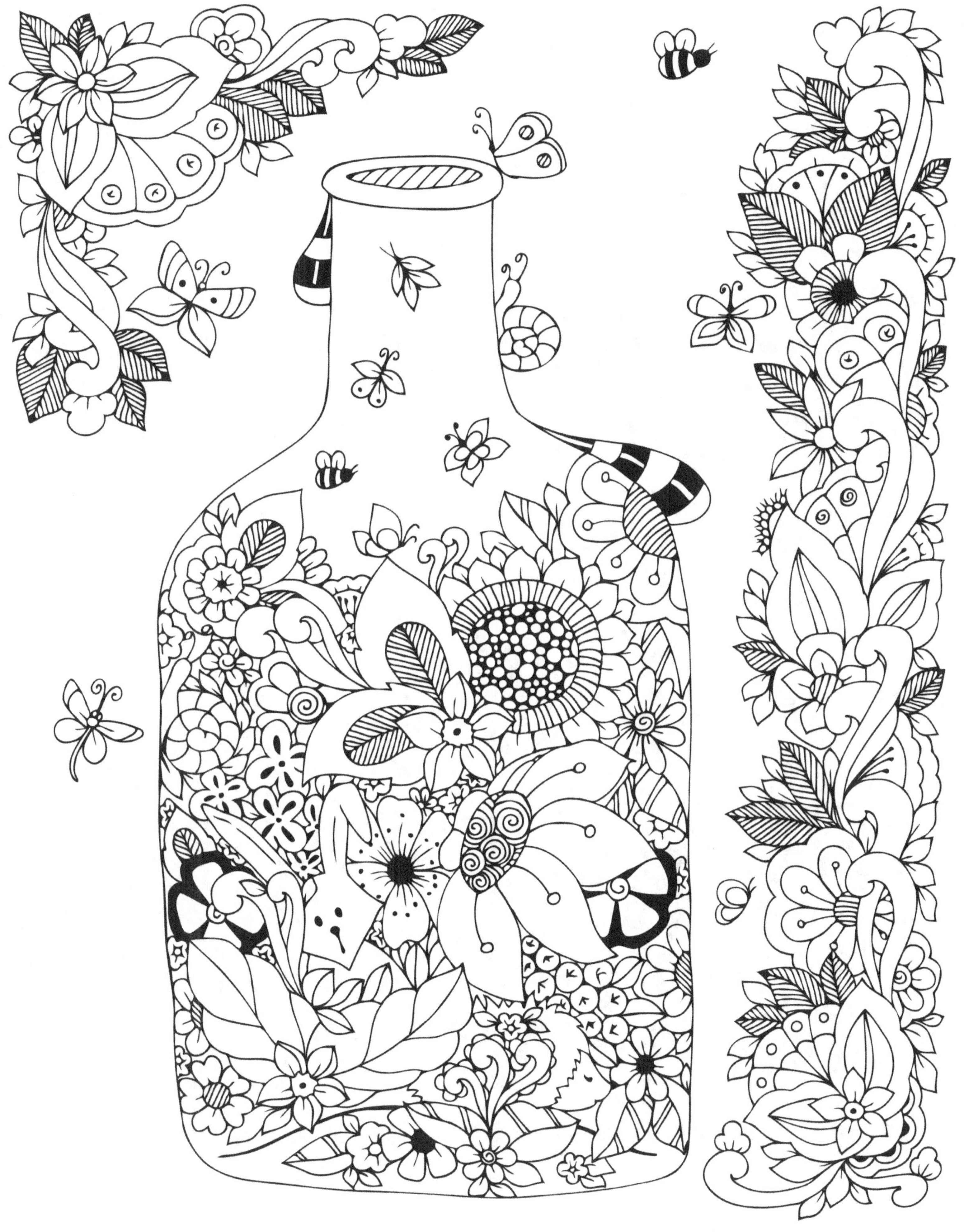

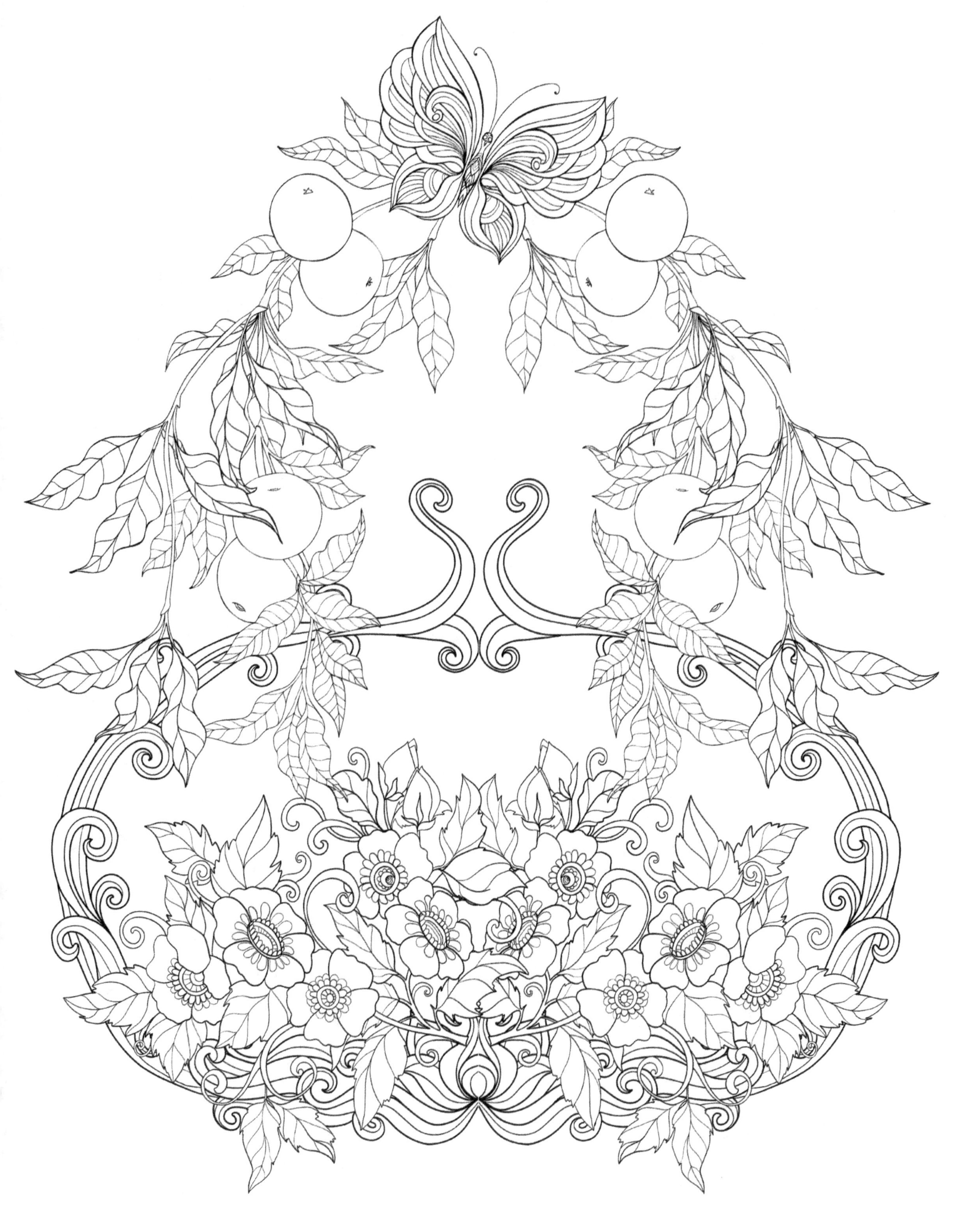

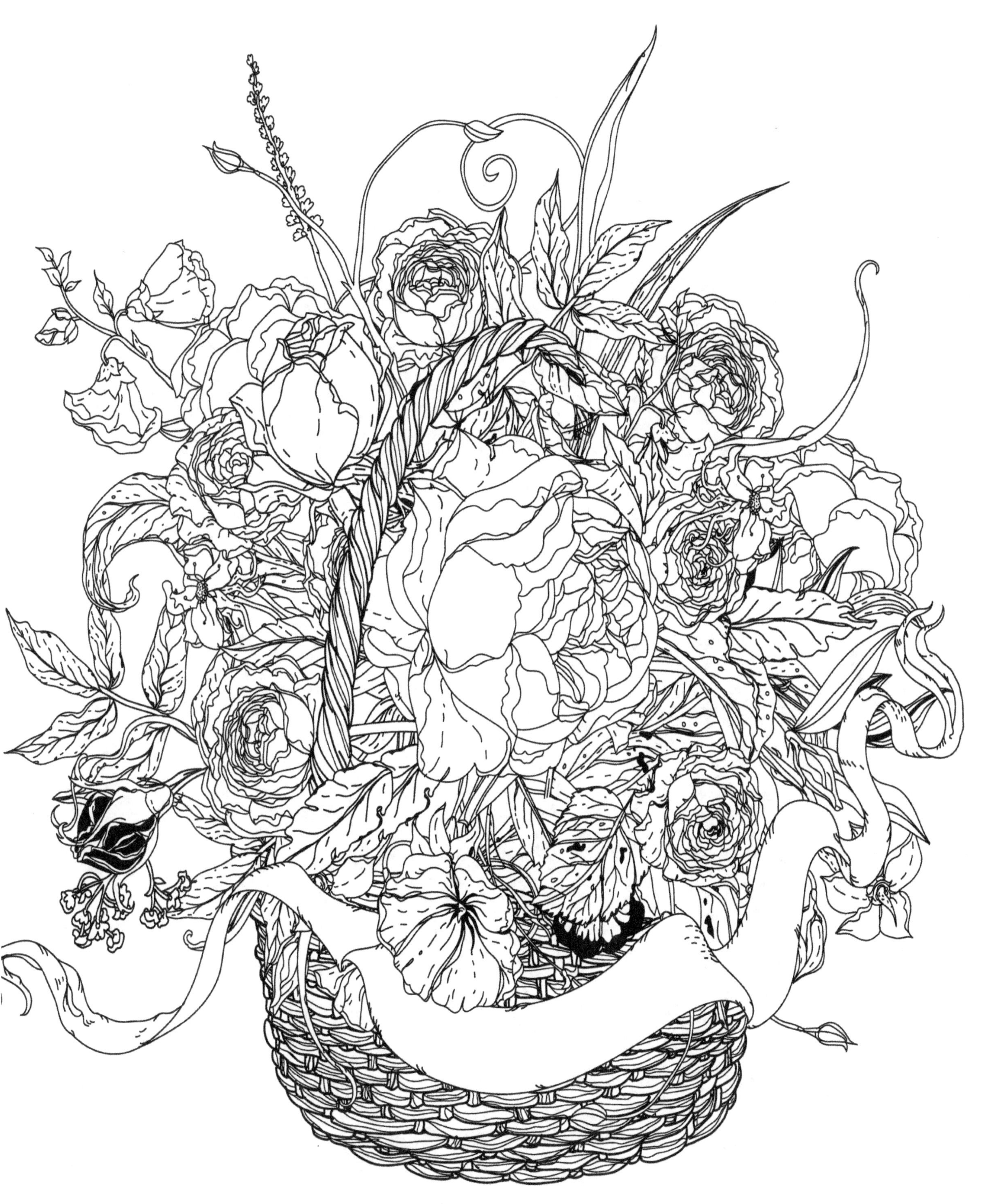

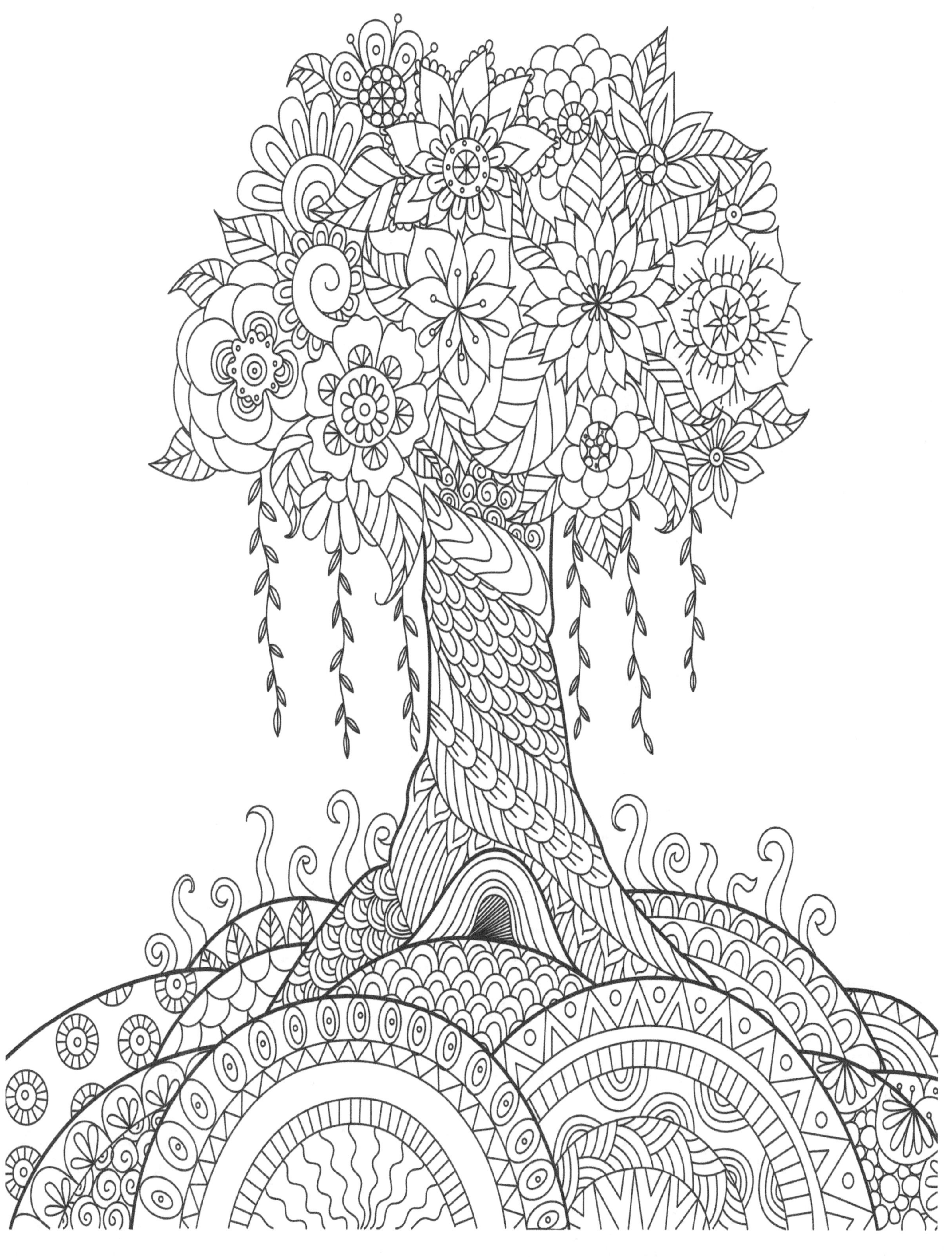

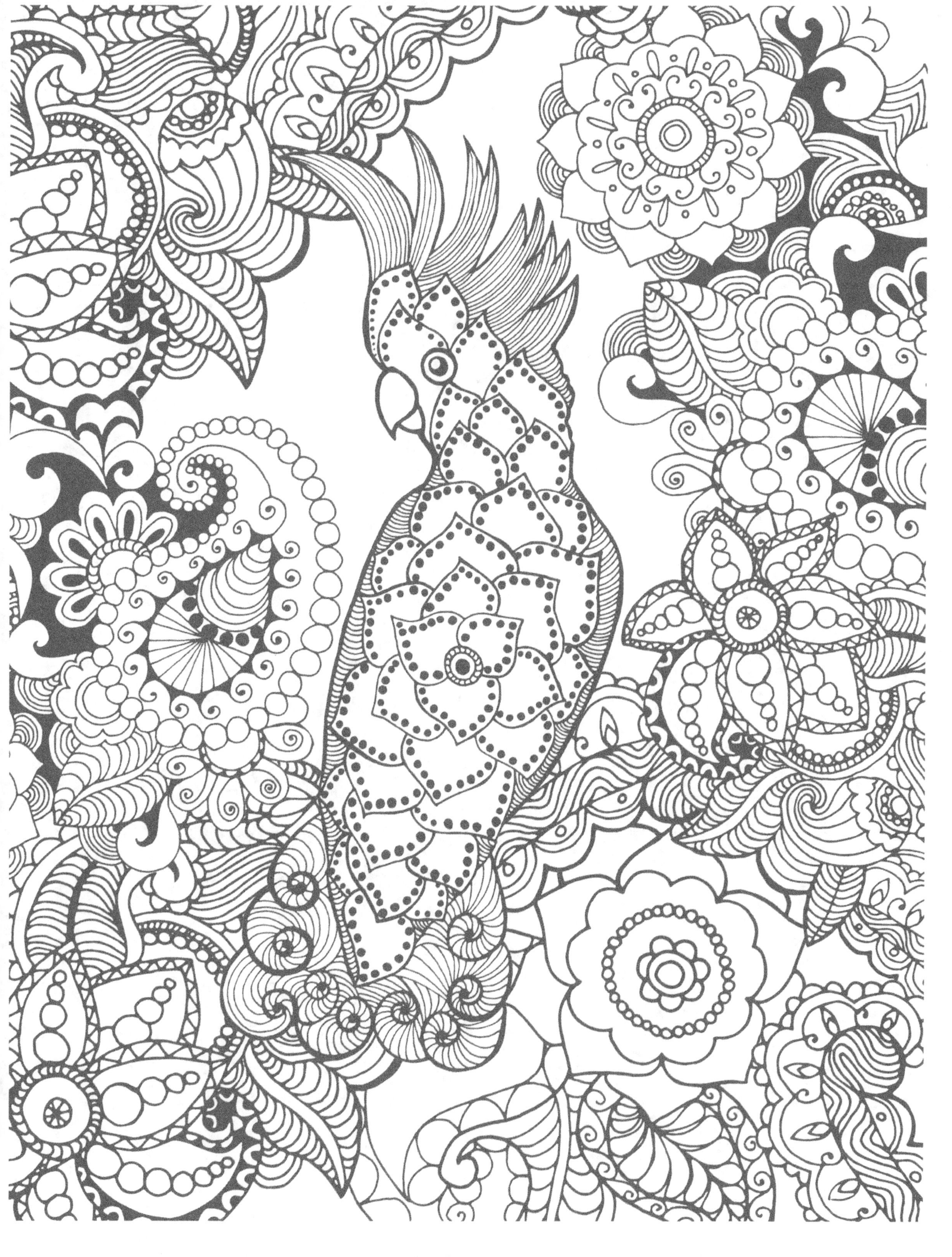

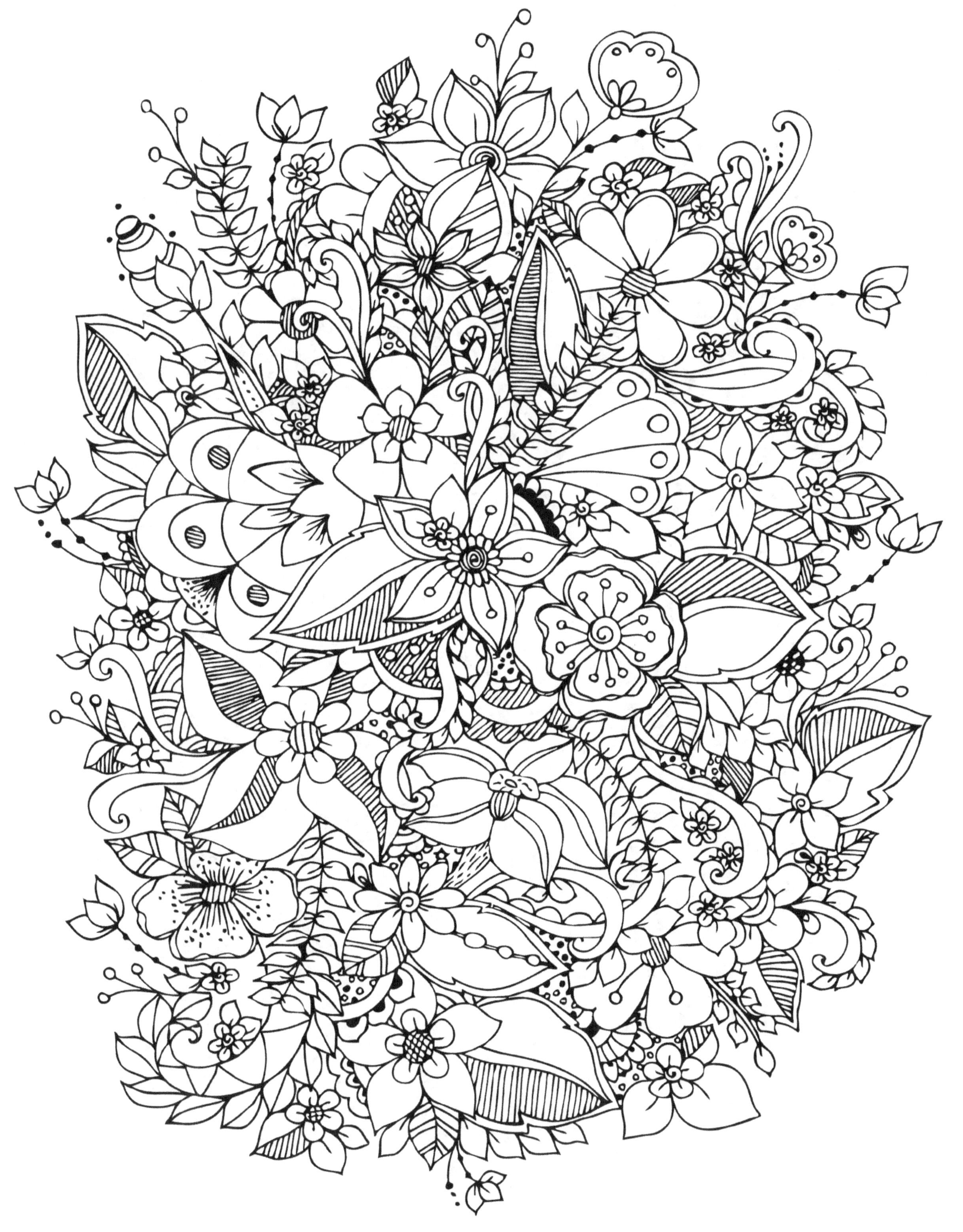

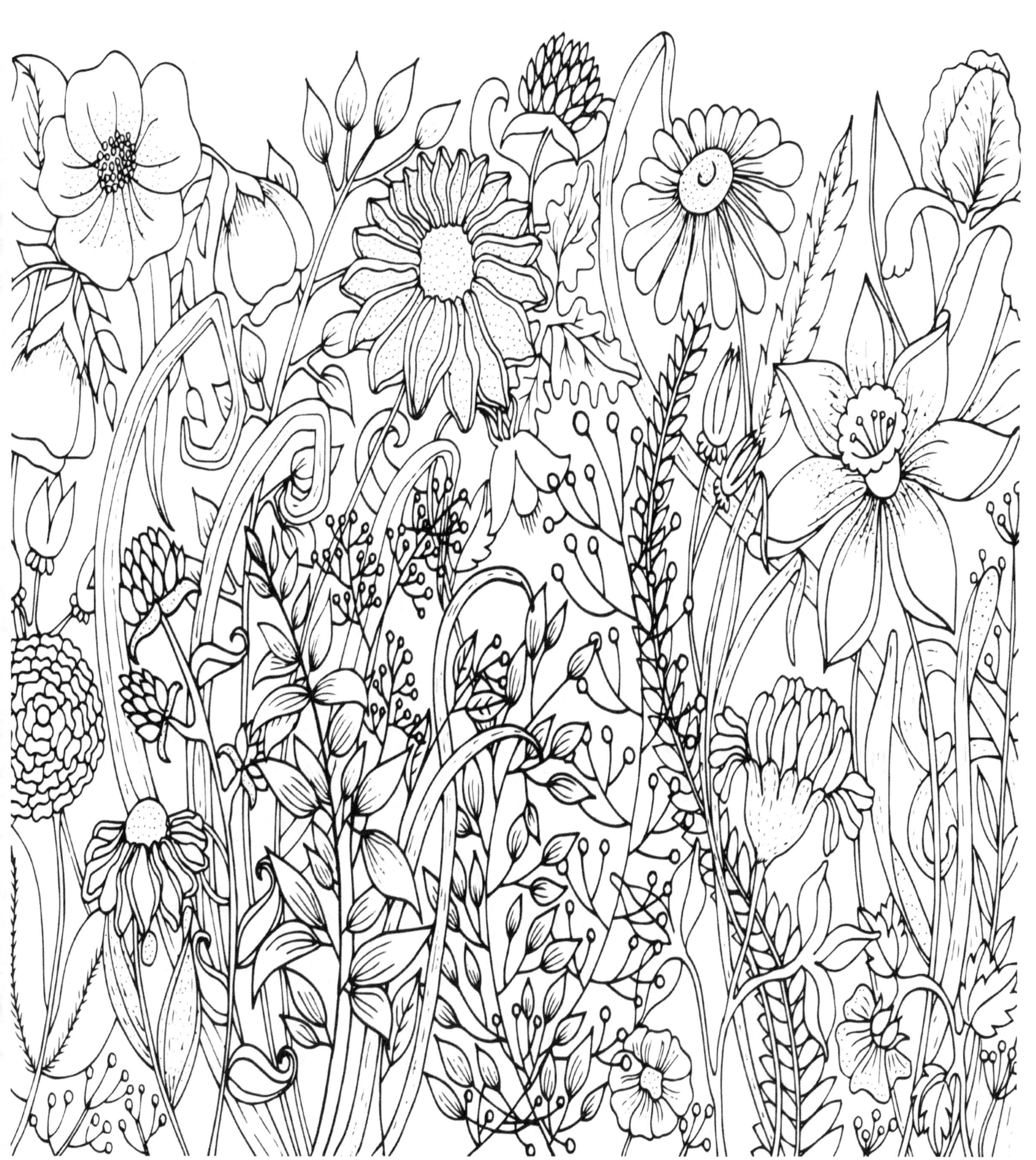

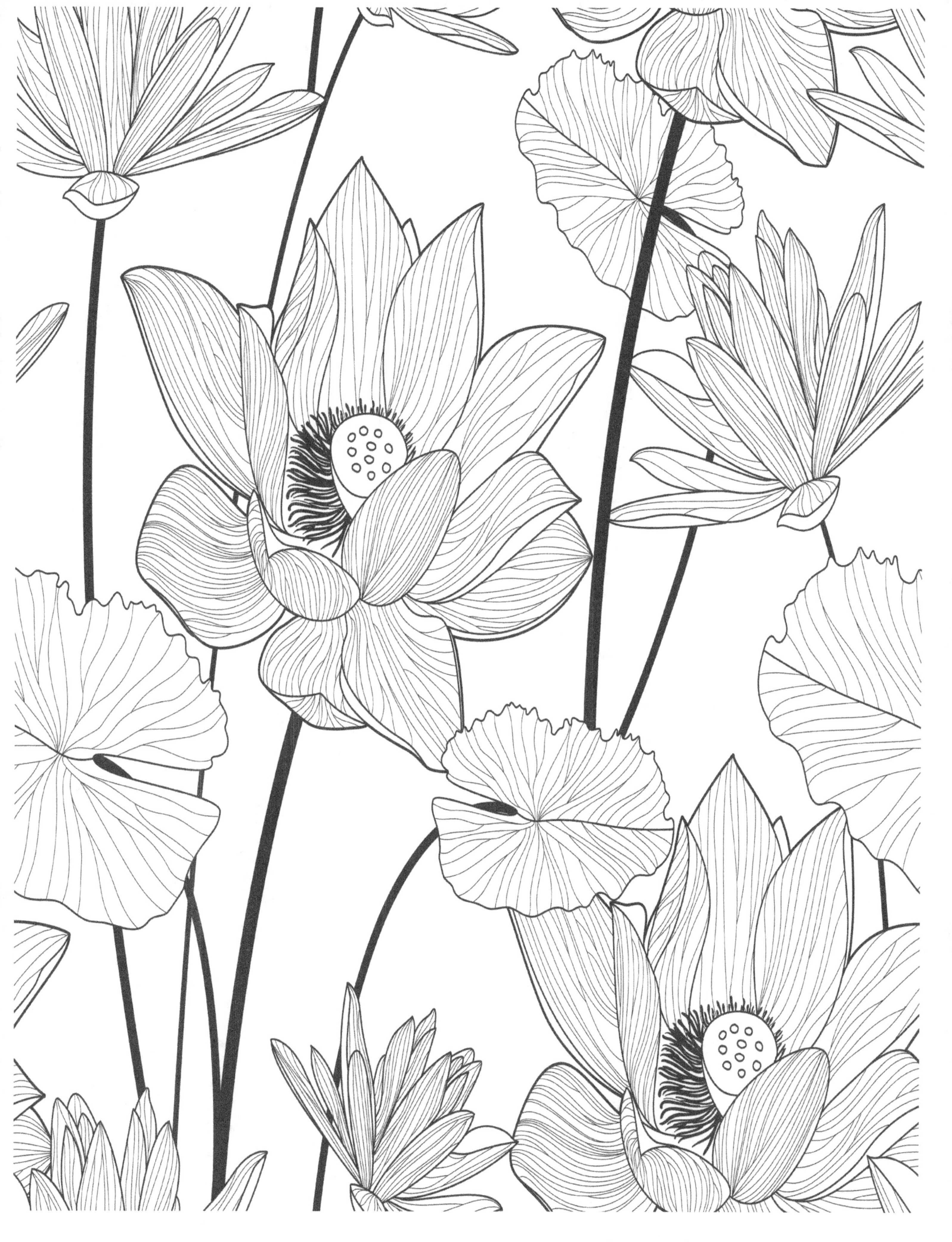

www.ingramcontent.com/pod-product-compliance
Lightning Source LLC
Chambersburg PA
CBHW080504030726
47592CB00011B/3237